Spiders & Insects

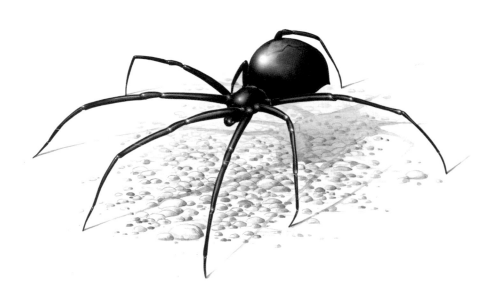

Steve Parker
Consultant: Dr Jim Flegg

Miles Kelly
PUBLISHING

First published in 2002 by
Miles Kelly Publishing Ltd
Bardfield Centre, Great Bardfield, Essex, CM7 4SL

Some material in this book can also be found in *100 Things You Should Know About Insects.*

Editor: Amanda Learmonth

Design: Debbie Meekcoms

Assistant Editor: Nicola Sail

British Library Cataloguing-in-Publication Data
A catalogue record for this book is available from the British Library

ISBN 1-84236-111-2

Printed in Hong Kong

www.mileskelly.net
info@mileskelly.net

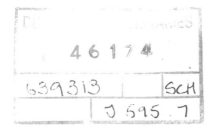

ACKNOWLEDGEMENTS

The Publishers would like to thank the following artists who have contributed to this book:

Susanna Addario (Scientific Illustration), Julian Baker Illustration, Andy Beckett (Illustration Limited), Dave Burroughs (Linda Rogers Associates), Chris Buzer (Studio Galante), Chris Daunt (Illustration Limited), Luca Di Castri (Studio Galante), Richard Draper, Mike Foster (Maltings Partnership), Wayne Ford, Chris Forsey, L.R. Galante (Studio Galante), Brooks Hagan (Studio Galante), Aziz Khan, Kevin Maddison, Janos Marffy, Massimiliano Maugeri (Studio Galante), Doreen McGuiness (Illustration Limited), Eric Robson (Illustration Limited), Martin Sanders, Sarah Smith (Linden Artists), Francesco Spadoni (Studio Galante), Rudi Vizi, Steve Weston (Linden Artists)

Computer-generated artwork by James Evans

Contents

Creepy-crawlies **4**

Insects everywhere! **6**

Flapping around **8**

Hop, skip and jump! **10**

Speedy bugs **12**

Swimmers and skaters **14**

Burrowing bugs **16**

Bites and stings **18**

Plant-munchers **20**

Insect homes **22**

Hide and seek **24**

Hard times **26**

What a noise! **28**

Is it an insect? **30**

What is a spider? **32**

The spider world **34**

A sting in the tail **36**

Nice or nasty? **38**

Index **40**

Creepy-crawlies

Insects form the largest of all animal groups, with millions of different kinds, or species. But not all creepy-crawlies are insects. Spiders belong to a different group called arachnids.

Millepedes belong to yet another group to spiders and insects.

Tarantulas have eight legs, like all arachnids.

Wood-ants are typical insects, with six legs and three body sections.

Insects everywhere!

Insects, such as the housefly, are among the most widespread of all animals. There are many other members of the fly group, such as bluebottles, horseflies, craneflies ('daddy-long-legs') and fruitflies. Other common insects include ladybirds, butterflies, ants and earwigs.

▼ *There are many different kinds of butterflies and moths. The white butterfly is not usually welcome in the garden. Their young, called caterpillars, eat the leaves of gardeners' plants.*

Spiders and insects

Insect-spotting

Have you seen any insects so
far today?

On a warm summer's day you
probably see many kinds of insects. On
a cold winter's day there are fewer insects
about. Most are hiding away or have not yet
hatched out of their eggs.

The scorpionfly
has a harmless
sting on a long,
curved tail.

Ants
are fine in the
garden or
wood, but are
pests in
the house.

The earwig
likes dark,
damp corners
– not ears
or wigs!

Flapping around

Most kinds of insects have two pairs of wings. An insect's wings are attached to the middle part of its body, the thorax. A large butterfly flaps its wings once or twice each second. Some tiny flies flap their wings about 1000 times each second.

▶ The clickbox is like a box with strong walls. Muscles pull to make the walls click in and out, which makes the wings flick up and down.

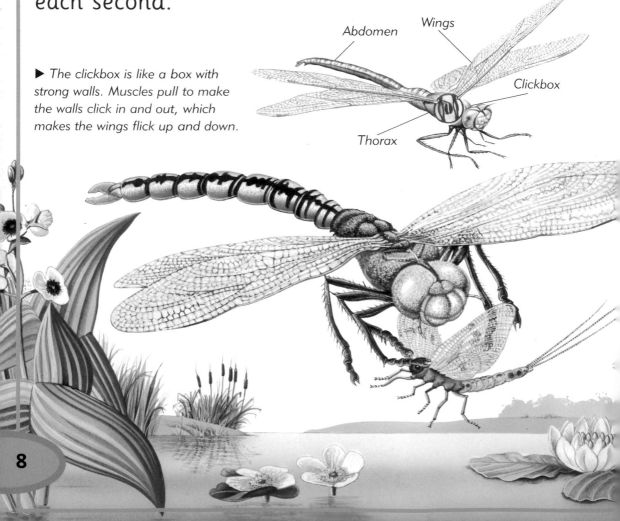

Abdomen

Wings

Clickbox

Thorax

8

Make a flapping fly!

You will need:

some stiff card • tissue paper
round-ended scissors • sticky tape

1. Ask an adult for help. Carefully cut out the card to make a box with two open ends, as shown.

2. Attach strips of stiff card to the sides to make struts for the wings. Make the rest of the wings from tissue paper.

3. Hold the box as shown. Move the top and bottom walls in, then out. This bends the side walls and makes the wings flap, just like a real insect.

The apollo butterfly is a strong flier, flapping over hills and mountains.

The firefly flashes bright lights as it flies to help attract a mate.

Mosquitoes are one of the smallest flying insects.

◀ The dragonfly is a fast and fierce flying hunter.

9

Hop, skip and jump!

Many insects move around mainly by hopping and jumping, rather than flying. They have long, strong legs and can leap great distances. They do this mainly to avoid enemies and escape from danger.

▼ *Grasshoppers have very long back legs. Some types can jump more than three metres.*

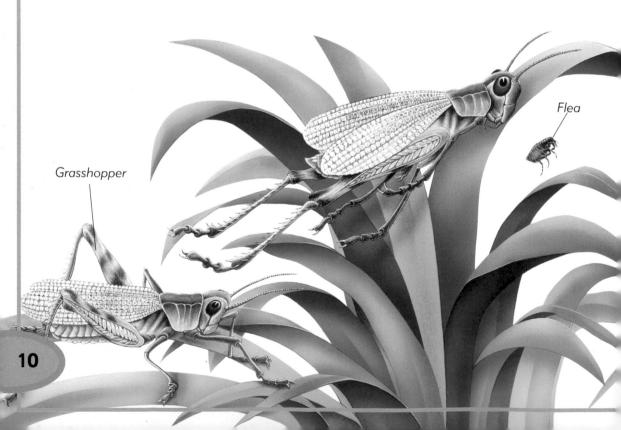

Grasshopper

Flea

Test your memory!

1. How many legs do arachnids have?

2. What is the name of a young butterfly?

3. Is the thorax the top, middle or bottom part of an insect's body?

4. Which insect flashes a bright light as it flies?

1. eight 2. caterpillar 3. the middle 4. the firefly

Fleas can jump the furthest for their body size.

Springtails jump with their tail, not their legs.

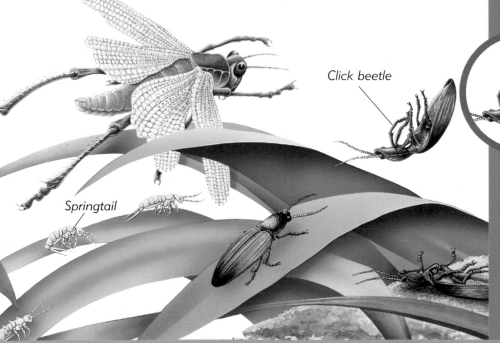

Click beetle

Springtail

Click beetles can flick themselves about 25 centimetres into the air.

11

Speedy bugs

Some insects hardly ever fly or leap. They prefer to run, and run, and run...all day, and even all night too. Among the champion insect runners are cockroaches. Most scurry speedily across the ground on long legs.

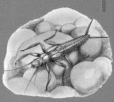

Stonefly nymphs run around on riverbeds searching for food.

The devil's coach-horse is a type of beetle that walks long distances to find food.

▲ Cockroaches have low, flat bodies. They can race into narrow holes, under stones and into furniture – and beds!

Bella's fun facts!

For its size, a green tiger beetle runs ten times as fast as a person! It runs about 60–70 centimetres per second. That is like a human sprinter running 100 metres in 1 second!

Swimmers and skaters

Many kinds of insects live underwater in ponds, streams, rivers and lakes. Some walk about on the bottom, such as the young, or nymphs, of dragonflies and damselflies. Others swim strongly using their legs as oars to row through the water.

Tadpoles

Gills

Damselfly nymph

Mayfly nymphs

Make an insect diving suit!

Young caddisflies, called nymphs, make tube-shaped cases, called caddis cases. These protect the nymph's body underwater. The nymph makes them from small bits collected from its surroundings.

You can make your own caddis case!

1. With the help of an adult, roll up a piece of cardboard to make a tube to wear on your forearm.
2. Stick bits, such as leaves or pebbles, on to the cardboard to build a giant caddis case.
3. Put your arm through the tube and wiggle your fingers like the caddis's head!

Mayfly nymphs have tails with feathery gills for breathing underwater.

Pondskater

Pondskaters are slim and light so they can walk on water.

Great diving beetle

Great diving beetles hunt tadpoles and baby fish.

15

Burrowing bugs

Soil is full of millions of creatures, and many are insects. Some are the wormlike young forms of insects, called larvae or grubs, as shown below. Others are fully grown insects, such as burrowing beetles, ants, termites and earwigs.

Cranefly ('daddy-long-legs')

Cranefly larva, leatherjacket

Bug quiz

Can you match the descriptions on the left
with the animals on the right?

A. Larger animal which
   eats soil creatures

B. Worm-like young insect

C. Another name for the
   leatherjacket

1. Larva

2. Mole

3. Cranefly
   larva

A and 2, B and 1,
C and 3

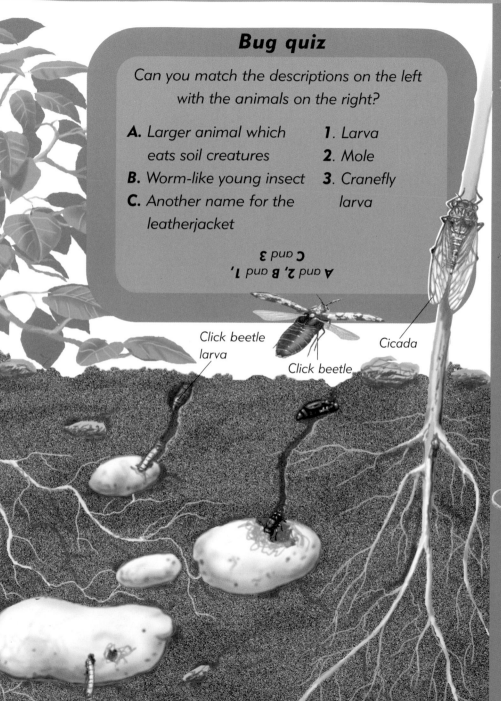

Click beetle
larva

Click beetle

Cicada

Cranefly larva
is called
leatherjacket
after its tough,
leathery skin.

Cicada larva
may live
underground
for more than
ten years.

Moles
feed on the
insects and
worms that
live in the soil.

17

Bites and stings

Most insects may be small, but they are among the fiercest hunters in the animal world. Many have mouthparts shaped like spears or saws, which they use for grabbing and tearing up victims. Some have very powerful bites and poison stings.

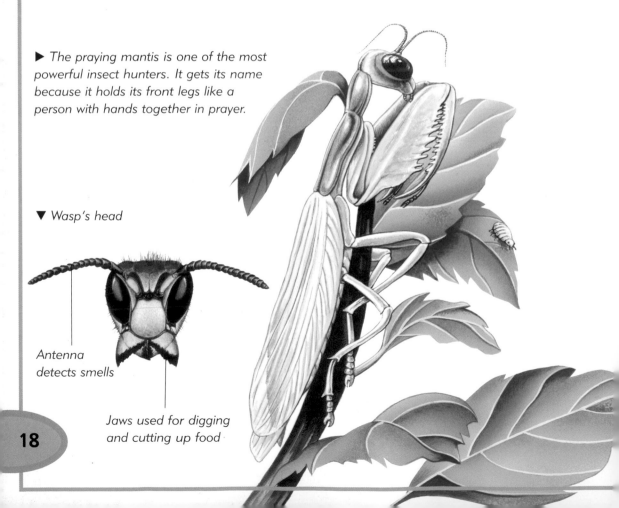

► The praying mantis is one of the most powerful insect hunters. It gets its name because it holds its front legs like a person with hands together in prayer.

▼ Wasp's head

Antenna detects smells

Jaws used for digging and cutting up food

Test your memory!

1. What kind of insect is the devil's coach-horse?
2. Which insect is one of the speediest runners?
3. Do gills allow an insect to eat or to breathe?
4. Which insect can walk on water?

3. to breathe 4. pondskater
1. a beetle 2. cockroach

The lacewing
is a fearsome
hunter of small
creatures.

**Bombardier
beetles**
squirt out a
horrible liquid
that stings their
enemies.

The hornet
is a large wasp
with a very
painful sting.

▼ The mantis stays perfectly still, then
when a victim comes near – SNAP!

19

Plant-munchers

About nine out of ten kinds of insects eat some sort of plant food. Many feed on soft, rich substances. These include the sap (liquid) in stems and leaves, the nectar in flowers and the soft flesh of squashy fruits and berries.

Elm beetle

Elm beetle larva

Mealy-bug

Furniture beetle

Woodworm (Furniture beetle larva)

Flower bug

▼ Insects are not fussy eaters. They feed on old bits of damp wood, brown leaves and rotting fruit.

Mealy-bugs lay their eggs in gaps in tree trunks and branches.

Capsid bug

Shieldbug

Woodworm eat their way through trees, houses and furniture.

Lacebug

Bella's fun facts!

Animal droppings are delicious to many kinds of insects. Various types of beetle lay their eggs in droppings, then the larvae hatch out and eat the dung!

Insect homes

Some insects live together in huge groups called colonies, which are like insect cities. There are four main types of insects which form colonies. One is the termites. The other three are bees, wasps and ants.

Royal chamber where the queen termite lays eggs

Male termite mates with queen

◄ Some kinds of termites make their nests in a huge pile of earth called a termite mound. It has many tunnels and chambers where the insects live.

Courtier workers look after the queen

Nursery termites care for eggs and larvae

Forager termites collect food

Cleaner termites repair the nest and get rid of wastes

▶ Some wasps build nests of paper, made from chewed-up bits of plants and wood.

Leaf-cutter ants make nests with leaves to grow fungus, which they eat.

Bees live in nests with around 50,000 others.

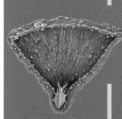

Ant-lion larva lives in sand or soil, waiting for its prey to pass.

Test your memory!

1. Finish the name of this insect predator: the praying.....?

2. What kind of insect is a hornet?

3. Does an insect's antenna let it breathe or smell?

4. Which worm-like creature likes to eat its way through wood?

1. mantis 2. a wasp 3. smell 4. woodworm

Hide and seek

Insects have some of the best types of camouflage in the whole world of animals. Camouflage is when a living thing is coloured and patterned to blend in with its surroundings. This makes it hard for predators (hunters) to see or find it. Or, if the insect is a predator itself, camouflage helps it to creep up on its prey.

▼ Stick and leaf insects look exactly like sticks and leaves.

▼ Many butterflies are brightly coloured. But the underside of their wings are dark – the same colour as the leaves.

Spiny green nymph

Rajah Brooke's bird-wing butterfly

Make a camouflage scene

1. Ask an adult to help. Carefully cut out a butterfly shape from stiff card. Colour it brightly with a bold pattern.

2. Cut out 10–20 leaf shapes from card. Colour them like your butterfly. Stick the leaves on a cardboard branch.

3. Your butterfly may seem far too bright to be camouflaged. But put the butterfly on your branch. See how well its camouflage works now!

The thornbug sits on a twig pretending to be a real thorn.

Shieldbugs have broad, flat bodies that look like the leaves around them.

Bird-dropping caterpillars look like bird's droppings, so no animal would want to eat them!

Green stick insect

Spiny green nymph

Rajah Brooke's bird-wing butterfly

Hard times

▼ Locusts (a type of grasshopper) migrate, or travel to warmer places. They grow in number and eat all the food in one area. Then they fly off to look for more.

The cold of winter or the dryness of hot weather are hard times for most animals, including insects.

How can they survive? One answer is to hibernate. Many insects find a safe place and go to sleep.

But these insects are not really asleep. They are simply too cold to move.

Death's-head hawkmoths fly south to Africa in winter.

Ladybirds hibernate under stones, bark or in grass.

Bella's fun facts!

Some insects migrate the wrong way! In Australia, bogong moths fly off to find warmer places. But some fly over the sea instead and can't find anywhere to land.

▶ Some insects migrate, or fly off, to warmer places in winter. The monarch butterfly spends the winter in warm parts of the USA and Mexico. Next spring they fly north again to feed and breed.

What a noise!

The tropical forest is warm and still — but far from quiet. Many insects are making chirps, buzzes, clicks, screeches, hums and other noises. Most are males, making their songs or calls to attract females at mating time.

Garden tiger moth

Giant wood wasp

Deathwatch beetle

Cockchafer

Click beetle

Screech beetle

Cicada

Test your memory!

1. Do ladybirds hibernate or migrate in winter?
2. Which butterflies spend the summer in parts of the USA and Mexico?
3. Which insect looks like a stick?
4. The four main types of insects which form colonies are termites, bees, ants and....?

1. they hibernate 2. monarch butterflies 3. stick insect 4. wasps

Crickets chirp by rubbing their wings together.

Cicadas are some of the noisiest insects.

Great green bush cricket

Click beetles make a clicking sound to warn off enemies.

Mole cricket

29

Is it an insect?

Are all minibeasts, bugs and creepy-crawlies truly insects? One way to tell is to count the legs. If a creature has six legs, it is an insect. If it has fewer or more, it is some other kind of animal. However, some young forms or larvae, like fly maggots, have no legs at all. But they develop into six-legged flies, and flies are certainly insects.

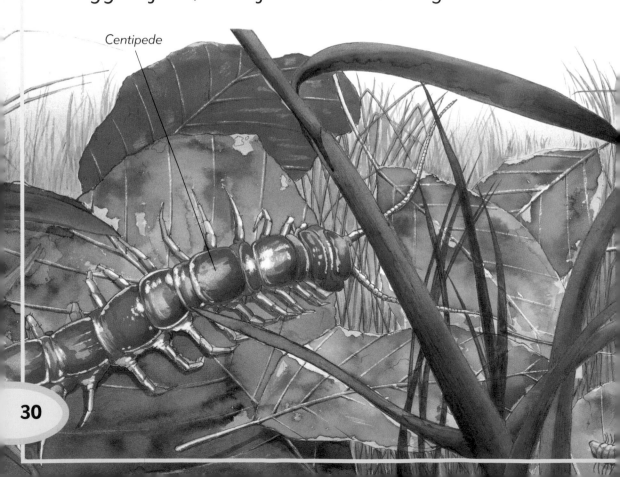

Centipede

Six legs or more?

Which of these minibeasts is an insect?

housefly   millepede
woodlouse   termite
centipede   butterfly

housefly, termite and butterfly
are all insects.

▼ Centipedes have lots of legs – usually over 30. Millepedes have 50 to 100 legs, maybe even more. Neither of them are insects.

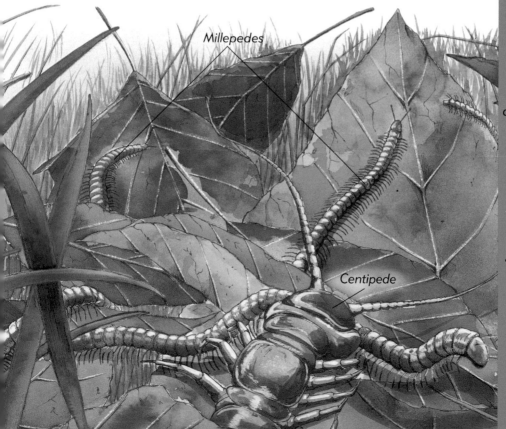

Millepedes

Centipede

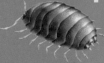

Ticks
have eight legs.
They suck blood
from animals.

Mites
belong to the
arachnid group,
as they have
eight legs.

The woodlouse
is a crustacean
– a cousin of
crabs and
lobsters.

What is a spider?

A spider has eight legs. So it is not an insect. It is a type of animal called an arachnid. All spiders are deadly hunters. They have large jaws which they use to kill their prey. They inject a poison to kill the victim. Like spiders, scorpions, mites and ticks have eight legs. So they are also arachnids.

▶ The Australian redback spider is one of the most deadly of a group called widow spiders.

Make a spiders web

You will need:

a piece of card • round-ended scissors
a reel of cotton • PVA glue

1. Ask an adult for help. Cut a large hole out of the card. Stretch a piece of cotton across the hole and stick both ends to the card.

2. Do the same again several times at different angles. Make sure all the threads cross at the centre of the hole.

3. Starting at the centre, glue a long piece of thread to each of the threads. Work your way round in a spiral until you reach the edge. That's the way that real spiders make webs!

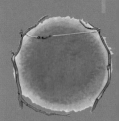

Stage one
A spider starts a web by building a bridge.

Stage two
It adds more threads to make a strong framework.

Stage three
The spider fills the frame with circular threads.

▼ The bolas spider catches insects flying past with its own kind of fishing line.

The spider world

Not all spiders catch their prey using webs.
Some spiders, such as the wolf spider, run fast and
chase tiny prey such as beetles and slugs. Others,
such as the trapdoor spider, hide away until an
animal passes, then jump out to grab their victim.

▼ Tarantulas are strong enough to catch big insects, such as this grasshopper, and even small birds.

▼ The gold leaf crab spider looks like a small crab. Here, it has caught a honeybee. Its poison paralyzes (freezes) the bee so it cannot escape.

The trapdoor spider *waits behind a door made of silk for its prey to pass.*

Wolf spiders *have long, strong legs for fast running.*

Bella's fun facts!

Tarantulas are huge spiders from South America and Africa. Stretch your hand out and it still would not be as big as some of these giants!

A sting in the tail

A scorpion has eight legs. It is not an insect. Like a spider, it is an arachnid. Scorpions live in warm parts of the world, such as rainforests and deserts. The scorpion has crablike pincers to grab its prey, and powerful jaws to chop it up.

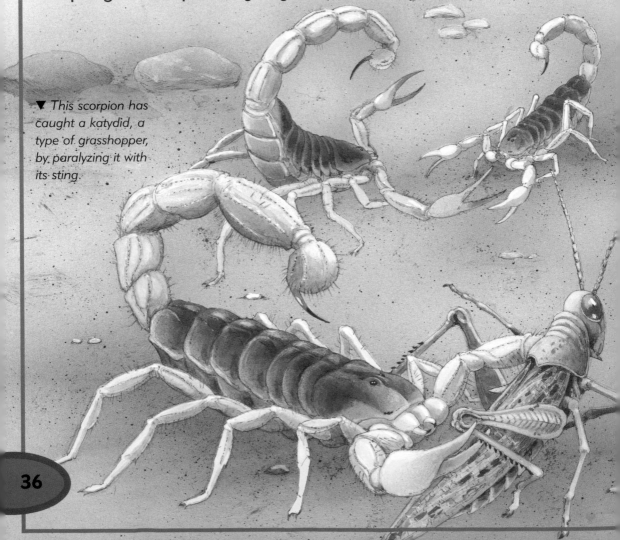

▼ This scorpion has caught a katydid, a type of grasshopper, by paralyzing it with its sting.

Spider scramble!

Unscramble the words below to find the names of four types of spider:

1. FLOW   **2. BRAC**

3. NATRALUTA   **4. WODIW**

1. wolf 2. crab 3. tarantula 4. widow

The sun-spider is a fierce hunter with a poisonous bite.

The false scorpion does not have a sting in its tail and is very small.

The black widow is a dangerous spider – its bite can kill people.

▲ The king crab has eight legs, so is an arachnid. It has a domed shell and spiky tail, but is harmless.

Nice or nasty?

Some insects are harmful – but others are very helpful. Butterflies and other insects visit flowers to collect nectar and pollen to eat. In the process they carry pollen from flower to flower. This is called pollination. It is needed so that the flower can form seeds or fruits.

Bees
make honey,
which is eaten
by many
animals,
including us!

Termites
can cause
damage to
wooden
buildings.

Bella's fun facts!

Certain kinds of termites eat
away at wood until it is almost
hollow. Then it
collapses into
a pile of dust
if anyone even
touches it!

▲ Spiders can be helpful to
gardeners. They catch lots of insect
pests, like flies, in their webs.

Index

A
abdomen **8**
antenna **18**
ants 6, **7**, 16,
   22
ant-lion larva **23**
arachnids 4, **5**, **31**,
   32, **36, 37**

B
bees 22, **23, 39**
beetles 16, 21, 34
   bombardier **19**
   click **11, 17, 29**
   deathwatch **28**
   devil's coach-horse
      13
   elm **20**
   furniture **20**
   great diving **15**
   green tiger 13
   screech **28**
bird-dropping
   caterpillar
   25
bluebottles 6
bugs 30
butterflies 6, 8,
   24, 38
   apollo **9**
   monarch **27**
   Rajah Brooke's
     bird-wing
     24–25
   white **6–7**

C D
caddisflies 15
camouflage 24
capsid bug **21**
caterpillars 6
centipedes **30–31**
cicada **17, 28–29**
clickbox **8**
cockchafer **28**
cockroach **12–13**
colonies 22
craneflies 6, **16**
crickets **28–29**
'daddy-long-legs' see
   craneflies
death's-head
   hawkmoth
   27
dragonfly **8–9**

E F G
earwig 6, **7**, 16
false scorpion **37**
firefly **9**
fleas **11**
flies 8, 30, **39**
flower bug **20**
fruitflies 6
garden tiger moth **28**
grasshoppers **10–11**,
   34, 36
great green bush
   cricket **29**
green stick insect **25**
grubs 16

H K
hibernation 26
honeybee **35**
hornet **19**
horseflies 6
houseflies 6
katydid **36**
king crab **37**

L
lacebug **21**
lacewing **19**
ladybirds 6, **27**
larvae **16–17**, 30
leaf-cutter ants **23**
leaf insects **24–25**
leatherjacket **16, 17**
locusts **26–27**

M N
maggots 30
mealy-bugs **20, 21**
migrate, migration 27
millepedes **5, 31**
mites **31**, 32
mosquitoes **9**
moths 6
mouthparts **18**
nests **22–23**
nymphs 14, 15
   damselfly 14
   dragonfly 14
   mayfly **14–15**
   spiny green **24–25**
   stonefly **13**

P Q
pollination 38
pondskaters **15**
praying mantis **18–19**
queen termite **22**

S
scorpions 32, **36–37**
scorpionfly **7**
shieldbug **21, 25**
spiders 4, 5, **38–39**
   Australian redback
     32–33
   black widow **37**
   bolas **33**
   gold leaf crab **35**
   tarantula **5, 34, 35**
   trapdoor 34, **35**
   wolf 34, **35**
springtails **11**
stick insects **24–25**
sun-spider **37**

T
termites 16, **22, 39**
thorax **8**
thornbug **25**
ticks **31**, 32

W
wasps **18**, 22, **23**
webs **33**, 34, **38–39**
wood-ants **5**
woodlouse **31**
woodworm **20, 21**